Carnation®

THE CARNATION EVAPORATED MILK COOKBOOK

SMITHMARK

INTRODUCTION

Welcome to our very special collection of kitchen-tested recipes for our oldest and most treasured product – Carnation evaporated milk! The original process for making this convenient milk, developed by Elbridge Amos Stuart in 1899, hasn't changed one iota since he set out to tell homemakers across the country about his wonderful product.

Very simply, evaporated milk begins with fresh whole milk, from which over half the water is removed through evaporation. It is then homogenized, placed in cans, and sterilized. No sweeteners are added.

Carnation evaporated milk remains today one of the original convenience foods. Did you know that you can use evaporated milk either as milk or in place of cream? When a recipe calls for milk, just mix Carnation evaporated milk with an equal amount of water. To replace cream, light cream or half and half, use Carnation evaporated milk as it is from the can. Its off-the-shelf convenience will also come in handy for an endless variety of soups, creamy sauces, desserts and candy recipes.

Get reacquainted with the wonderful versatility of Carnation evaporated milk with the delightful assortment of recipes in this book, from salads and dressing to entrees, candies, breads and scrumptious desserts. Here are just a few to whet your appetite: Chicken Cilantro Bisque, Fish with Three Pepper Sauce, Homemade Ice Cream, Cinnamon Swirl Bread and Baked Lemon Sponge Pudding.

If you're watching calories, reach for Carnation evaporated skimmed or lowfat milk for a lower fat and calorie alternative. The calorie and fat conscious eaters will find recipes which include these healthier options; recipes including Turkey Santa Fe, Whole Wheat Apple Muffins, Country-style Harvest Bread, and Light Apricot Mousse.

For over 90 years enthusiastic cooks have enjoyed the wonderful simplicity and convenience of Carnation evaporated milk. This delightful selection of recipes shows just how many ways you can enjoy it, now and for many years to come.

CLB 2595
©1992 Colour Library Books Ltd, Godalming, Surrey, England.
Text ©1992 Nestlé Food Company.
All rights reserved.
This edition published in 1992 by
SMITHMARK Publishers Inc., 112 Madison Avenue, New York, NY 10016
Printed and bound in Singapore.
ISBN 0 8317 3190 7

SMITHMARK books are available for bulk sales promotion and premium use. For details write or telephone the Manager of Special Sales, SMITHMARK Publishers Inc., 112 Madison Avenue, New York, NY 10016. (212) 532-6600.

Carnation and Libby's are registered trademarks of Société des Produits Nestlé.

Carnation®
EVAPORATED
MILK

CREAMY BASIL PASTA SALAD

Makes 7 to 8 cups

This colorful favorite will be a hit packed for lunches or for your next family picnic. No one will guess that it's lower in saturated fat, cholesterol and salt.

10oz uncooked rotini pasta (twists)
2 cups sliced vegetables
½ cup undiluted CARNATION Evaporated Skimmed Milk
½ cup vegetable oil
2 tbsps white wine vinegar
2 tbsps chopped sun-dried tomatoes (optional)
1 tbsp chopped fresh basil or 1½ tsps dried basil, crushed
½ tsp seasoned or garlic salt
¼ tsp cracked fresh pepper
Fresh basil (optional)

1. Cook pasta according to package directions; drain and chill.

2. In medium saucepan, steam assorted vegetables; drain and chill.

3. In blender container, place evaporated skimmed milk, oil, vinegar, tomatoes, basil, salt and pepper; process 2 to 5 seconds. Do not overprocess. Chill.

STEP 3

4. To serve, combine pasta and vegetables in a large bowl, toss with chilled dressing, and garnish with fresh basil, if desired.

STEP 2

STEP 4

Cook's Notes

⌚ TIME: Preparation takes about 30 minutes, chilling takes about 1 hour.

❓ VARIATION: Type of pasta and choice of vegetables can be changed for a totally different look.

⃝ SERVING IDEA: Sprinkle with freshly grated Parmesan cheese.

🍳 COOK'S TIP: Rotini is a type of spiral pasta and is available in both dried and fresh forms.

CHEESY GARDEN VEGETABLE MEDLEY
Makes 2 servings

No one will ever miss the butter or salt in this tasty cheese sauce made with evaporated skimmed milk and reduced-fat cheese.

---

3 to 4 cups fresh vegetables
½ cup undiluted CARNATION Evaporated
    Skimmed Milk, divided
1 tbsp plus 2 tsps all-purpose flour
¼ cup water
1 tsp country Dijon-style mustard
½ cup (2oz) shredded reduced-fat Cheddar cheese
1 tbsp toasted sesame seeds

---

1. In medium saucepan, steam vegetables until tender.

in remaining evaporated skimmed milk, water and mustard. Cook over medium heat, stirring constantly, until mixture comes to a boil and thickens.

STEP 2

3. Add cheese and stir until melted.

STEP 1

2. Meanwhile, in small saucepan, whisk small amount of evaporated skimmed milk into flour. Stir

STEP 3

4. Serve over hot vegetables, and sprinkle with sesame seeds.

Cook's Notes

⏱ TIME: Preparation takes about 15 minutes, cooking takes about 15 minutes.

❓ VARIATION: Choose from carrots, summer squash, broccoli, cauliflower or asparagus.

🍽 SERVING IDEA: Appropriate as a main dish or side dish accompaniment.

👨‍🍳 COOK'S TIP: Frozen vegetables may be used to speed up preparation time.

CHICKEN CILANTRO BISQUE

Makes about 4 servings

This delicious lower calorie classic is not only healthy, but is easy to make with a blender or food processor.

2 medium (6oz) boneless, skinless chicken breast halves
2½ cups low-sodium chicken broth
½ cup cilantro leaves
½ cup sliced green onion
¼ cup sliced celery
1 large clove garlic, minced
½ tsp ground cumin seed
⅓ cup all-purpose flour
1½ cups (12oz can) undiluted CARNATION Evaporated Skimmed Milk
Freshly ground pepper to taste

1. Cut chicken into bite-size pieces.

2. In large saucepan, combine chicken, broth, cilantro, green onion, celery, garlic, and cumin. Bring to a boil. Cover, reduce heat and boil gently for 15 minutes.

3. Pour soup into blender container and add flour. Cover and blend, starting at low speed, until smooth.

STEP 3

4. Pour mixture back into saucepan. Cook over medium heat, stirring constantly, until mixture comes to a boil and thickens. Remove from heat. Gradually stir in evaporated skimmed milk. Reheat just to serving temperature. Do not boil. Season with pepper.

STEP 2

STEP 4

Cook's Notes

⏱ TIME: Preparation takes about 10 minutes, cooking takes about 30 minutes.

🅾 SERVING IDEA: Garnish with diced tomatoes, onions or peppers, and fresh cilantro leaves, and serve with a loaf of crusty bread.

❓ VARIATION: Turkey breast can be substituted for the chicken.

📖 COOK'S TIP: Cilantro is also known as coriander or Chinese parsley. To store, place in refrigerator with stems in a glass of water and a plastic bag over the leaves. Change water every day and it should stay fresh for a week.

GREAT AMERICAN CHOWDER

Makes about 7 cups

This hearty chowder is a meal in itself, and a great way to use up leftovers. Serve it with a crisp green salad and crusty bread.

---

6 slices bacon, diced
1 tbsp vegetable oil
1½ cups chopped onions
¼ cup chopped celery
¼ cup all-purpose flour
3 cups (1½lbs) peeled potatoes, diced
1¾ cups water
1⅔ cups (14½oz can) chicken broth
1 cup cubed, cooked ham, chicken or turkey
1 cup mixed vegetables
½ tsp salt
⅛ tsp ground pepper
1 cup undiluted CARNATION Evaporated Milk
Parsley (optional)

---

1. Cook bacon until crisp, drain on paper towels, and set aside.

2. Heat oil in large saucepan and sauté onions and celery until soft.

3. Stir in flour. Add potatoes, water, broth, ham, vegetables, salt, and pepper. Bring to a boil. Reduce heat and boil gently for 20 minutes or until potatoes are tender, stirring occasionally.

STEP 3

4. Stir in evaporated milk and half of the bacon. Heat to serving temperature. Garnish with remaining bacon and parsley, if desired.

STEP 2

STEP 4

Cook's Notes

⏱ TIME: Preparation takes about 25 minutes, cooking takes about 30 minutes.

❓ VARIATION: Use any leftover cooked meats and a variety of vegetables, including corn, cut green beans, peas and carrots or lima beans.

⊙ SERVING IDEA: Bacon may be sprinkled on top of chowder instead of stirred in.

🍳 COOK'S TIP: Frozen vegetables may be used to speed up preparation time.

MUSHROOM FONDUTA

Makes 2¾ cups

Fondue is back in vogue! What a great way to start your next 'get-together'.

1 clove garlic, peeled and halved
3 egg yolks
⅔ cup <u>undiluted</u> CARNATION Evaporated Milk
⅓ cup water
2 tbsps dry white wine
1 cup chopped, fresh mushrooms
2 tbsps butter or margarine
2 tbsps all-purpose flour
3 cups (12oz) shredded Fontina cheese
Pumpernickel, French or Italian bread, cubed

1. Rub inside of fondue pot or chafing dish with the cut surface of garlic; discard.

2. In small bowl, beat egg yolks, mix in evaporated milk, water, and wine, then set aside.

STEP 2

3. In medium saucepan, sauté mushrooms in butter over medium heat for about 5 minutes. Stir

in flour then gradually stir in egg mixture. Cook over medium heat, stirring constantly, until mixture just comes to a boil and thickens.

STEP 3

4. Reduce heat, add cheese and stir until cheese is melted, but <u>do not</u> boil.

STEP 4

5. Pour into fondue pot or chafing dish and keep warm. Serve with bread cubes.

Cook's Notes

TIME: Preparation takes about 15 minutes, cooking takes about 20 minutes.

SERVING IDEA: In addition to bread, serve with a selection of colorful, blanched, sliced vegetables such as carrots, cauliflower, celery, broccoli, zucchini, and peppers.

VARIATION: Gruyère cheese may be substituted for the Fontina.

COOK'S TIP: Fontina and Gruyère are both semi-soft, creamy cheeses with a delicate, sweet-nutty flavor.

CREAMY DILL AND CRAB DIPS

Makes 1²/₃ cups dill dip and 2 cups crab dip

These tasty dips, served with a variety of vegetables, are sure to please either as appetizers or party fare.

Dill Dip

¼ cup cider vinegar
2 tsps sugar
1 tsp seasoned salt
1 tsp dried dill weed, crushed
1 cup <u>undiluted</u> CARNATION Evaporated Milk
1 cup mayonnaise
1 tbsp finely chopped green onion
1 tbsp finely chopped parsley
Fresh dill (optional)

Crab Dip

1 package (8oz) cream cheese, softened
¼ cup undiluted CARNATION Evaporated Milk
¾ cup (6oz can) flaked crab meat, drained
1 tbsp grated onion
1 tbsp lemon juice
1 tsp Worcestershire sauce
¼ tsp garlic salt
Lemon slices and parsley (optional)

1. To make the dill dip, combine vinegar, sugar, salt and dill weed in small bowl, gradually stir in evaporated milk and continue to stir until smooth and thickened. Blend in mayonnaise, green onion and parsley.

2. Cover and chill thoroughly to blend flavors. Garnish with fresh dill before serving, if desired.

STEP 1

3. To make the crab dip, combine cream cheese and evaporated milk in mixing bowl until smooth and creamy. Stir in crab meat, grated onion, lemon juice, Worcestershire sauce and garlic salt, mixing well.

STEP 3

4. Cover and chill thoroughly to blend flavors. Garnish with lemon and parsley before serving, if desired.

Cook's Notes

TIME: Preparation takes about 10 minutes for each dip, chilling takes about 1 hour.

COOK'S TIP: Dips can be prepared well in advance and refrigerated until serving time.

SERVING IDEA: Serve with a choice of blanched snowpeas, green beans, broccoli, cauliflower, mushrooms, carrot and celery sticks, potato chips or assorted crackers.

BROILED FISH WITH THREE PEPPER SAUCE

Makes 4 servings

The bright colors and sweet taste of red, green and yellow peppers make this a memorable sauce. Made with evaporated lowfat milk, it is lower in fat, cholesterol and salt.

2 tbsps olive oil
1 cup julienne-cut red, green, and yellow peppers
1 cup sliced mushrooms
½ cup chopped onion
1 clove garlic, minced
2 tbsps all-purpose flour
¾ cup <u>undiluted</u> CARNATION Evaporated Lowfat Milk
¼ cup water
2 tbsps dry white wine
¼ tsp salt
1 tbsp chopped fresh basil leaves or ½ tsp dried basil leaves, crushed
12oz fresh fish fillets or steaks
Fresh basil (optional)
Blanched snowpeas (optional)

1. In medium skillet, heat 1 tablespoon of the olive oil and sauté the peppers, mushrooms, onion and garlic over medium heat for about 6 minutes or until excess moisture is evaporated. Stir in flour and cook, stirring constantly for 1 minute.

2. Gradually add evaporated lowfat milk, water, wine and salt. Heat, stirring constantly, until mixture comes to a full boil and thickens. Stir in basil and keep warm.

STEP 2

3. Lightly brush both sides of fish with remaining oil. Place on broiler rack, tucking under any thin ends. Broil 6 inches from heat without turning for about 4 to 6 minutes, or until fish flakes easily with a fork.

STEP 3

4. Serve warm sauce over fish, garnished with extra basil and blanched snowpeas, if desired.

Cook's Notes

⏱ TIME: Preparation takes about 15 minutes, cooking takes about 15 minutes.

❓ VARIATION: Fish or chicken stock can be used instead of wine.

◎ SERVING IDEA: Serve with brown rice and garnish with lemon slices.

🍳 COOK'S TIP: The leanest types of fish include black sea bass, cod, flounder, haddock, halibut, perch and red snapper.

TURKEY SANTA FE

Makes 4 servings

Flavors of the Southwest – chiles, cilantro, garlic and cumin – mingle to make this delicious, creamy sauce.

1⅔ cups water
⅛ tsp salt
⅔ cup brown rice
10oz raw turkey breast slices
⅔ cup undiluted CARNATION Evaporated
    Skimmed Milk
⅓ cup reduced-salt chicken broth
2 tbsps plus 1 tsp all-purpose flour
3 tbsps canned, mild diced green chiles
2 tbsps chopped cilantro leaves
2 tbsps sliced green onion
1 clove garlic, cut in half lengthwise
½ tsp ground cumin
¼ tsp salt
Fresh cilantro leaves (optional)

---

1. In small saucepan, combine water and salt, and bring to a boil. Stir in rice and reduce heat to lowest setting. Cover and cook about 40 minutes until rice is cooked and moisture is absorbed.

2. Meanwhile, lightly pound turkey slices. Spray non-stick skillet with no stick cooking spray. Heat skillet over medium-low heat, add turkey slices and sauté about 2 minutes on each side.

3. Arrange cooked rice on serving platter with turkey slices on top, cover and keep warm.

STEP 2

4. To make sauce, combine evaporated skimmed milk, broth, flour, chiles, cilantro, green onion, garlic, cumin and ¼ teaspoon salt in blender container. Cover and blend until smooth.

STEP 4

5. Pour into medium saucepan. Cook over medium-low heat, whisking constantly, until mixture comes to a boil and thickens. Serve over turkey and rice. Garnish with fresh cilantro leaves, if desired.

Cook's Notes

🕐 TIME: Preparation takes about 10 minutes, cooking takes about 40 minutes.

❓ VARIATION: Turkey and sauce may be served over pasta instead of rice.

⊙ SERVING IDEA: Sauce can also be served over chicken or firm fleshed fish.

🍳 COOK'S TIP: Make the entire meal in the time it takes to cook the brown rice.

CHICKEN BREASTS WITH PROVOLONE SAUCE

Makes 4 servings

Great for entertaining. Easy Cordon Bleu with a twist – the ham is placed on top of chicken and the cheese is in the sauce.

2 tbsps all-purpose flour
1 tsp dried tarragon leaves, crushed
½ tsp salt
¼ tsp white pepper
4 (about 1 pound) boneless, skinless chicken breast halves
2 tbsps butter or margarine
4 slices (2oz) boiled ham
2 tsps all-purpose flour
⅓ cup dry white wine
⅔ cup undiluted CARNATION Evaporated Milk
1 cup (4oz) shredded provolone cheese
Fresh parsley (optional)

1. In plastic bag, combine 2 tablespoons flour, tarragon, salt and pepper, then add chicken. Shake well to coat.

STEP 1

2. In medium skillet, melt butter. Sauté chicken over medium heat until golden and cooked through. Remove to heated platter.

STEP 2

3. Cut ham into strips, and heat 2 to 3 minutes in same skillet. Place over chicken and keep warm.

4. Stir 2 teaspoons flour into drippings in skillet, blending well. Stir in wine and gradually add evaporated milk. Cook over medium heat until mixture just comes to a boil and thickens. Add cheese, and mix until melted.

STEP 4

5. Ladle sauce over chicken and ham. Garnish with fresh parsley, if desired.

Cook's Notes

🕐 TIME: Preparation takes about 10 minutes, cooking takes about 15 minutes.

❓ VARIATION: Turkey, pork or veal cutlets can be used instead of chicken, and prosciutto can replace ham.

◯ SERVING IDEA: Serve over wild rice for a crunchy, interesting texture.

🍳 COOK'S TIP: If using prosciutto, reduce salt to ¼ teaspoon.

EASY STRAWBERRY ICE CREAM

Makes about 1 quart

Only four ingredients are needed to make this refreshing ice cream. Frozen berries make it easy and are available year round.

2⅓ cups undiluted CARNATION Evaporated Milk
1¾ cups (16oz package) frozen strawberries with
    sugar, thawed
¼ cup sugar
2 tbsps lemon juice

1. Place evaporated milk, strawberries, sugar and lemon juice in blender container and purée until well blended.

STEP 1

2. Pour into ice cream maker; freeze according to manufacturer's instructions. (Texture will be soft – for a firmer texture, place in home freezer for 1 to 2 hours.) Place in a plastic container and store in freezer until required.

STEP 2

STEP 2

Cook's Notes

🕐 TIME: Preparation takes 10 minutes, freezing takes about 30 minutes for a soft consistency.

❓ VARIATION: Any type of berry may be used. If using fresh berries, increase sugar. After pureeing, strain mixture to remove seeds before freezing.

🍽 SERVING IDEA: Create an impressive dessert by serving a scoop of ice cream on a Chocolate Caramel Brownie base, then top with Rich Fudge Sauce.

👨‍🍳 COOK'S TIP: Garnish with fresh strawberry fans. Select firm berries with stems and starting at tip, cut into thin slices almost to stem. Spread slices apart to form fan shape.

FAMOUS FIVE MINUTE FUDGE

Makes 2 pounds

This versatile and easy candy can be served as is or dressed up for special occasions.

---

2 tbsps butter or margarine
⅔ cup <u>undiluted</u> CARNATION Evaporated Milk
1⅔ cups sugar
½ tsp salt
2 cups (4oz) miniature marshmallows
1½ cups semisweet chocolate chips or pieces
1 tsp vanilla extract
½ cup chopped nuts

---

1. Grease an 8-inch square pan.

2. In medium saucepan, combine butter, evaporated milk, sugar and salt. Bring to a boil over medium heat, stirring constantly. Boil 4 to 5 minutes, stirring constantly. Remove from heat.

3. Stir in marshmallows, chocolate chips, vanilla and nuts. Stir vigorously for 1 minute until marshmallows melt and blend.

STEP 3

4. Pour into pan, cool, and cut into squares.

STEP 2

STEP 4

Cook's Notes

TIME: Preparation takes 15 minutes, cooking takes 5 minutes, plus cooling time.

VARIATION: To make Fudge Rolls, spread about 1 cup chopped toasted nuts on waxed paper. Pour cooked fudge mixture over nuts. As fudge cools, form into a roll. Slice.

SERVING IDEAS: Fudge may be cut into various shapes such as squares, and triangles, or use a small heart-shaped cookie cutter for that 'special' person.

COOK'S TIP: Place in colorful candy papers for any festive occasion.

TOASTED ALMOND TRUFFLES
Makes about 2 dozen

These dainty morsels are wonderful during the holiday season or any time of year! Best made ahead to allow flavors to blend.

½ cup undiluted CARNATION Evaporated Milk
¼ cup sugar
2 cups (11½oz package) milk chocolate morsels
1 tsp almond extract or almond liqueur
½-¾ cup finely chopped almonds, toasted

1. In small, heavy-gauge saucepan, combine evaporated milk and sugar. Cook over medium heat until mixture comes to a full boil, and continue to boil for 3 minutes, stirring constantly. Remove from heat.

STEP 1

2. Add chocolate morsels and almond extract. Stir until chocolate is melted and mixture is smooth. Chill for 45 minutes.

STEP 2

3. Form into 1-inch balls, working quickly to prevent melting. Roll in toasted almonds and chill until ready to serve.

STEP 3

Cook's Notes

⏱ TIME: Preparation takes about 20 minutes, chilling takes about 45 minutes.

❓ VARIATION: Be creative and try various liqueurs including orange, hazelnut and chocolate flavors in place of the almond extract.

⭕ SERVING IDEA: Place in colorful candy papers for holiday gift-giving.

🍳 COOK'S TIP: Vary the outside coating before serving – roll in grated semisweet baking chocolate, sifted powdered sugar or in a mixture of sifted cocoa and powdered sugar.

WHOLE WHEAT APPLE MUFFINS

Makes 12 muffins

These nutritious, lower fat muffins, created with fresh apples, apple juice and spices, and topped with cinnamon-sugar, are packed with flavor.

1¼ cups all-purpose flour
¾ cup whole wheat flour
⅓ cup sugar
1 tbsp baking powder
1 tsp ground cinnamon
½ tsp ground ginger
1 egg
⅔ cup undiluted CARNATION Evaporated Lowfat Milk
⅓ cup apple juice
¼ cup vegetable oil
1¼ cups (1 large) peeled, finely diced apple
1 tbsp cinnamon-sugar
Fresh mint (optional)

STEP 2

1. Preheat oven to 400°F. Grease or paper-line 12 muffin cups.

2. In medium bowl, combine flour, sugar, baking powder, cinnamon and ginger. In small bowl, lightly beat egg. Stir in evaporated lowfat milk, apple juice and oil. Add liquid ingredients to dry ingredients and stir just until moistened. Fold in apples.

3. Spoon batter into muffin cups. Sprinkle cinnamon-sugar over batter. Bake for 25 minutes or until toothpick inserted in center comes out clean. Remove from pan and cool on wire rack. Decorate with mint before serving, if desired.

STEP 2

STEP 3

Cook's Notes

⏱ TIME: Preparation takes about 10 minutes, baking takes about 25 minutes.

❓ VARIATION: The spices may be varied – try cinnamon, cloves and nutmeg or cinnamon and allspice.

⭕ SERVING IDEA: Serve muffins in pretty napkin-lined basket for breakfast or brunch.

👨‍🍳 COOK'S TIP: To freeze muffins, wrap securely in foil or place in freezer bag. Seal well, label and date.

QUICK STREUSEL COFFEE CAKE

Makes one cake

This cake may look complicated but it's not! With packaged baking mix and a fluted tube pan it is both quick and easy.

Streusel
½ cup packed brown sugar
½ cup chopped nuts
2 tsps ground cinnamon

Batter
3 cups buttermilk baking mix
1 cup granulated sugar
⅓ cup butter or margarine
1 egg
1 cup underlined CARNATION Evaporated Milk
⅓ cup water

Frosting
¾ cup powdered sugar
1 tbsp lemon juice

1. Preheat oven to 350°F. Generously grease and flour an 8-cup fluted tube pan.

STEP 3

2. To make the streusel, combine brown sugar, nuts and cinnamon in small bowl.

3. To make the batter, combine baking mix and granulated sugar in large bowl, and using a pastry blender, cut in butter until the mixture is crumbly.

4. In small bowl, lightly beat egg. Stir in evaporated milk and water. Add liquid ingredients to dry ingredients and stir just until moistened (batter will be lumpy).

5. To assemble the cake, spoon half of batter into tube pan, sprinkle half of streusel over batter, and repeat with remaining batter and streusel. Bake for 35 to 40 minutes, or until toothpick inserted, comes out clean. Cool for 10 minutes, then invert onto serving plate and allow to cool.

STEP 5

6. Combine powdered sugar and lemon juice in a small bowl, then drizzle the frosting over the cooled cake.

Cook's Notes

⏱ TIME: Preparation takes about 10 minutes, baking takes about 25 minutes.

❓ VARIATION: Can also be baked in 12 x 8 x 2-inch baking dish.

◯ SERVING IDEAS: Serve for breakfast, brunch or anytime snacking. Great with coffee or tea.

EASY PECAN STICKY BUNS

Makes 12 buns

Surprise family and friends with these quick breakfast treats – turn them upside down to reveal the crunchy, sticky pecans.

Pecan Sauce
¾ cup packed brown sugar
⅓ cup butter or margarine
¼ cup water
½ cup coarsely chopped pecans

Cinnamon-Sugar
2 tbsps granulated sugar
1 tsp ground cinnamon

Dough
2 cups all-purpose flour
1 tbsp baking powder
¾ tsp salt
1 cup undiluted CARNATION Evaporated Milk
⅓ cup vegetable oil

1. To make the pecan sauce, combine brown sugar, butter, water and pecans in small saucepan. Boil gently for 10 minutes. Pour into 9-inch round layer cake pan and set aside.

STEP 1

2. For the cinnamon-sugar, combine granulated sugar and cinnamon in small bowl and set aside.

3. Preheat oven to 400°F.

4. To make the dough, combine flour, baking powder and salt. Add evaporated milk and oil, blend well and form into a ball.

5. On a lightly floured surface, roll dough into 12 x 10-inch rectangle, sprinkle with cinnamon-sugar and roll up starting at longer side. Cut into 12 slices.

STEP 5

6. Place dough slices on top of pecan mixture in cake pan, spacing them evenly. Bake for 20 to 25 minutes or until golden brown. Invert onto serving plate.

STEP 6

Cook's Notes

⏱ TIME: Preparation takes 16 minutes, baking takes about 20 minutes.

❓ VARIATION: Traditionally pecans are used, but any nut meats would be delicious – try walnuts.

GOLDEN POUND CAKE WITH LEMON CUSTARD SAUCE

Makes one 10-inch tube cake

Pound cake is extremely versatile – serve with the sauce to impress family and friends, or pack for a lunchtime treat.

Cake
3 cups sifted cake flour
1½ tsps baking powder
¼ tsp mace
¼ tsp salt
1 cup butter or margarine, softened
1½ cups sugar
1 tsp vanilla extract
3 eggs
½ cup <u>undiluted</u> CARNATION Evaporated Milk

Lemon Custard Sauce
¾ cup sugar
2 tsps cornstarch
¾ cup <u>undiluted</u> CARNATION Evaporated Milk
½ cup water
2 egg yolks, beaten
2 tbsps lemon juice
1 tsp grated lemon zest

1. Preheat oven to 350°F. Grease and flour a 10-inch tube pan.

2. In medium bowl, combine flour, baking powder, mace and salt.

3. In large mixer bowl, cream butter, sugar, and vanilla until light and fluffy. Add eggs, one at a time, beating well after each addition.

4. Add dry ingredients alternately with small amounts of evaporated milk, beating well after each addition.

STEP 4

5. Spoon into tube pan and smooth. Bake for 55 to 60 minutes or until wooden skewer, when inserted, comes out clean. Cool in pan on wire rack for 10 minutes. Invert onto rack to cool completely.

STEP 5

6. To make the lemon custard sauce, combine sugar and cornstarch in a small saucepan and gradually stir in evaporated milk, water and beaten egg yolks. Cook over medium-low heat, stirring constantly until mixture comes to a boil and thickens. Cool slightly, then stir in lemon juice and lemon zest. Serve sauce, warm, with the pound cake.

Cook's Notes

TIME: Preparation takes about 16 minutes, baking takes about 1 hour, plus cooling time.

VARIATION: Sauce may be omitted and powdered sugar sifted over the cake.

SERVING IDEA: Sweetened, whipped cream may be added either in place of, or in addition to, the lemon sauce.

COOK'S TIP: Cake is very good when lightly toasted and buttered.

FAMOUS PUMPKIN PIE

Makes one 9-inch pie

This traditional pie is America's all-time favorite, served plain or with sweetened whipped cream.

1 unbaked 9-inch (4-cup volume) pie crust
2 eggs
1¾ cups (16oz can) LIBBY'S Solid Pack Pumpkin
¾ cup sugar
½ tsp salt
1 tsp ground cinnamon
½ tsp ground ginger
¼ tsp ground cloves
1½ cups (12oz can) undiluted CARNATION
 Evaporated Milk

1. Preheat oven to 425°F. Prepare pie crust.

2. In large bowl, lightly beat eggs. Mix in pumpkin, sugar, salt, cinnamon, ginger, cloves and evaporated milk, and pour into unbaked pie crust.

STEP 2

When using metal or foil pie pan, bake on preheated baking sheet. When using glass or ceramic pie plate, do not use baking sheet.

3. Bake for 15 minutes. Reduce temperature to 350°F. Bake an additional 40 to 50 minutes, or until knife inserted near center comes out clean. Top cooled pie as desired.

STEP 2

STEP 3

Cook's Notes

🕐 TIME: If using a ready-made crust, preparation takes about 5 minutes, baking about 1 hour, plus cooling time.

❓ VARIATION: For a decorative crust, cut small leaf shapes, triangles, squares etc. from pastry trimmings, or braid narrow strips of pastry. Attach to edge of crust with a little cold water before filling and baking.

⬚ SERVING IDEA: For a topping, combine 1½ cups sour cream, 2 tbsps sugar, 1 tsp vanilla extract, and ½ tsp grated orange zest; mix well. Spread over top of hot pumpkin pie.

🍽 COOK'S TIP: To prevent crust from over-browning, place foil collar around edge halfway through baking.

PRALINES AND CREAM PIE

Makes one 9-inch pie

A creamy, maple-flavored custard filling is topped with a crunchy pecan layer in this irresistible pie.

1 unbaked 9-inch (4-cup volume) pie crust
1 cup undiluted CARNATION Evaporated Milk
4 eggs
⅓ cup butter or margarine, melted
1 cup granulated sugar
¾ cup packed light brown sugar
3 tbsps all-purpose flour
1 tsp vanilla extract
1½ cups pecans, coarsely chopped
Sweetened whipped cream or ice cream (optional)

1. Preheat oven to 350°F. Prepare pie crust.

2. In blender container, combine evaporated milk, eggs, butter, sugar, flour and vanilla, and blend until smooth. Stir in pecans. Pour into unbaked pie crust.

STEP 2

3. Bake for 30 to 40 minutes, or until knife inserted comes out clean. Cool completely on wire rack before cutting. Refrigerate until ready to serve. Serve with sweetened whipped cream or ice cream, if desired.

STEP 2

STEP 3

Cook's Notes

⏱ TIME: Preparation takes 8 minutes, baking takes about 30 minutes, plus cooling time.

◎ SERVING IDEAS: Cool the pie completely before serving. Top with sweetened whipped cream or ice cream for that special occasion.

🍞 COOK'S TIP: Pie may be made several hours ahead but be sure to keep it refrigerated until serving time.

CHEESY SOUTHWEST CORNBREAD
Makes 9 servings

This chile-cheese combination has a traditional, Southwest flavor.

1½ cups yellow cornmeal
½ cup all-purpose flour
3 tbsps sugar
1 tbsp baking powder
½ tsp baking soda
1 tsp salt
¼ cup vegetable shortening
1 egg
1 cup undiluted CARNATION Evaporated Milk
½ cup water
5 tsps vinegar
⅔ cup (4oz can) diced green chiles
1 cup (4oz) shredded Cheddar cheese

1. Preheat oven to 425°F. Generously grease 9-inch square baking pan.

2. In large bowl, combine cornmeal, flour, sugar, baking powder, baking soda and salt; mix well.

With pastry blender, cut in shortening until mixture is crumbly.

3. In small bowl, beat egg. Mix in evaporated milk, water and vinegar. Add liquid ingredients to dry ingredients. Stir in chiles and cheese, and mix just until blended.

STEP 3

4. Pour into baking pan and bake for 20 to 25 minutes. Cut into squares and serve warm.

STEP 2

STEP 4

Cook's Notes

⏱ TIME: Preparation takes about 15 minutes, baking takes about 20 minutes.

❓ VARIATION: One half cup of thinly sliced green onions may be substituted for the green chiles.

◎ SERVING IDEAS: Serve with any entrée, though especially good with chili, barbecued meats, baked beans, thick soups of salads.

👨‍🍳 COOK'S TIP: Leftovers can be split, toasted and used as a base for creamed chicken, ham or tuna.

ZUCCHINI SPICE BREAD

Makes two 9 x 5-inch loaves

A rich, moist loaf that is delicious spread with butter or cream cheese and served for tea, or to accompany soup or salad.

4 cups all-purpose flour
2 cups sugar
2 tsps ground cinnamon
1½ tsps baking powder
1 tsp salt
3 eggs
1½ cups shredded unpeeled zucchini
¾ cup undiluted CARNATION Evaporated Milk
⅔ cup water
¼ cup vegetable oil
2 tsps vanilla extract
½ cup chopped nuts

1. Preheat oven to 325°F. Grease two 9 x 5-inch loaf pans.

2. In large bowl, combine flour, sugar, cinnamon, baking powder, baking soda and salt.

3. In medium bowl, beat eggs, then add zucchini, evaporated milk, water, oil and vanilla. Stir liquid ingredients into dry ingredients just until blended. Fold in nuts.

STEP 3

4. Spoon batter into 2 loaf pans. Bake for 60 to 70 minutes, or until toothpick inserted in center comes out clean. Cool 10 minutes. Remove from pans and cool on wire racks.

STEP 2

STEP 4

Cook's Notes

⏱ TIME: Preparation takes about 20 minutes, baking time 70 minutes, plus cooling time.

❓ VARIATION: Substitute 1½ cups shredded carrot for zucchini.

◎ SERVING IDEA: For a breakfast treat, toast lightly and serve warm.

COUNTRY-STYLE HARVEST BREAD

Makes one 9 x 5-inch loaf

This delightful, hearty bread uses evaporated skimmed milk, and is loaded with oats, fresh apples and chopped nuts, making it the perfect high fiber, lower fat treat.

1½ cups quick-cooking oats
¾ cup undiluted CARNATION Evaporated Skimmed Milk
¼ cup water

Topping
1 tbsp quick-cooking oats
1 tbsp chopped walnuts

Batter
1½ cups all-purpose flour
⅓ cup packed dark brown sugar
1 tbsp pumpkin pie spice
1 tsp baking powder
1 tsp baking soda
¼ tsp salt
1 egg
¼ cup molasses
3 tbsps vegetable oil
1 cup Jonathan or Granny Smith apples, peeled, cored and chopped
¼ cup chopped walnuts
Apple slices and mint leaves (optional)

1. Preheat oven to 350°F. Grease a 9 x 5-inch loaf pan.

2. In medium bowl, soak oats in evaporated skimmed milk and water, then set aside for 10 minutes.

3. To make the topping; combine oats and walnuts in a small bowl and set aside.

STEP 2

4. To make the batter; combine flour, sugar, pie spice, baking powder, baking soda and salt in large bowl. In another bowl, beat egg, mix in molasses and oil, and oat-milk mixture. Add liquid ingredients to dry ingredients, mixing well. Stir in apples and walnuts.

5. To assemble, pour batter into loaf pan, sprinkle topping over batter, and bake for 40 to 45 minutes, or until toothpick comes out clean. Cool 15 minutes. Remove from pan and cool completely on wire rack. Garnish with apple slices and mint leaves, if desired.

STEP 5

Cook's Notes

TIME: Preparation takes about 20 minutes, baking takes about 40 minutes.

VARIATION: Use a different type of nut meat, and change the spices.

SERVING IDEA: Appropriate as a breakfast, lunch or brunch bread.

COOK'S TIP: Can be made ahead and frozen for use later. Also good toasted.

CHEESE SWIRL YEAST BREAD

Makes two 9 x 5-inch loaves

Nothing beats the smell of fresh bread baking – try this easy, savory bread which has a delicious cheesy flavor in every slice.

---

1 envelope active dry yeast
½ cup warm water (105-115°F)
⅔ cup <u>undiluted</u> CARNATION Evaporated Milk
⅓ cup water
2 tbsps sugar
1¼ tsps salt
3 to 3¾ cups all-purpose flour
¾ cup (3oz) shredded Cheddar cheese

---

1. In large bowl, dissolve yeast in ½ cup warm water. Stir in evaporated milk, ⅓ cup water, sugar and salt. Stir in about 3 cups flour.

2. On lightly floured surface, knead dough until smooth and elastic, working in additional flour as necessary. Place dough in large, greased bowl, turning to coat all sides. Cover and let rise in a warm, draft-free place for about 1 hour, or until doubled in bulk. Punch down dough, divide in half.

3. On lightly floured surface, roll out each half of dough into 12 x 8-inch rectangle. Sprinkle cheese over surface of dough. Roll up tightly starting at short end and seal edges.

STEP 3

4. Place each roll in greased 9 x 5-inch loaf dish. Cover and leave to rise in a warm, draft-free place until doubled in bulk.

STEP 4

5. To bake; preheat oven to 350°F and bake for 20 to 25 minutes, or until golden brown. Remove from pans and cool on wire racks.

Cook's Notes

⏱ TIME: Preparation takes about 20 minutes, rising takes about 3 hours, and baking takes about 20 minutes.

❓ VARIATION: To make cinnamon swirl bread, add ½ cup each chopped pecans and raisins with flour. Omit cheese. Sprinkle a combination of 4 tablespoons sugar and ½ teaspoon ground cinnamon over surface of dough rectangles before rolling up.

⭕ SERVING IDEA: Great accompaniment for any entrée, soup or salad.

🍳 COOK'S TIP: Bread freezes well – seal in plastic freezer bags, label and date.

SLICE 'N' BAKE SPICE COOKIES

Makes 30 cookies

These rich cookies of Danish origin are a favorite of all ages. They travel well for picnics, lunches or in the mail!

4 cups all-purpose flour
1 cup packed brown sugar
1 tbsp baking powder
1 tsp baking soda
1 tsp salt
1 tbsp ground cinnamon
½ tsp ground cloves
½ tsp ground nutmeg
1 cup butter or margarine, softened
1 cup undiluted CARNATION Evaporated Milk
1 cup almonds, chopped

1. In large mixer bowl, combine flour, sugar, baking powder, baking soda, salt, cinnamon, cloves and nutmeg. Add butter and evaporated milk, and mix well. (The dough will be very stiff; if necessary, use hands to mix.) Stir in nuts.

2. Divide dough into 2 portions, and shape each into approximately 2½-inch rolls. Cover with plastic wrap, and chill.

STEP 2

3. To bake, preheat oven to 350°F. Cut dough into ¼-inch slices. Place on baking sheet and bake for 15 minutes or until lightly browned. Cool slightly. Remove from baking sheet and cool on wire racks.

STEP 1

STEP 3

Cook's Notes

🕐 TIME: Preparation takes 10 minutes plus chilling time. Baking takes 15 minutes.

❓ VARIATION: For different shaped cookies, rolls may be flattened slightly before chilling and slicing.

◎ SERVING IDEAS: Good served with a pot of tea or coffee and fresh fruit, if desired. Also great with a glass of milk.

📖 COOK'S TIP: Pecans or walnuts may be substituted for the almonds.

CHOCOLATE CARAMEL BROWNIES

Makes 48 brownies

Nuts, chocolate and caramel make an irresistible combination. Prepared cake mix makes it easy!

1 package (18oz approx.) devil's food or chocolate
    cake mix
1 cup finely chopped nuts
½ cup butter or margarine
½ cup undiluted CARNATION Evaporated Milk
35 (10oz) light caramels
⅓ cup undiluted CARNATION Evaporated Milk
1 cup (6oz package) semisweet chocolate chips or
    pieces

1. Preheat oven to 350°F. Grease a 13 x 9 x 2-inch baking pan.

2. In large bowl, combine cake mix and nuts. With pastry blender, cut in butter until mixture is crumbly. Stir in ½ cup evaporated milk. Spread half of batter into baking pan. Bake for 15 minutes.

STEP 2

3. In small saucepan, combine caramels and ⅓ cup evaporated milk. Cook over low heat, stirring occasionally, until caramels are melted.

STEP 3

4. Sprinkle chocolate chips over baked layer. Drizzle with caramel syrup and spread carefully to cover chocolate layer. Drop remaining batter by heaping teaspoon over caramel.

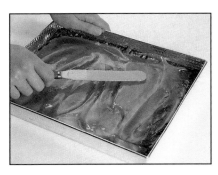

STEP 4

5. Bake 20 to 25 minutes longer (top layer will be soft). Cool completely before cutting.

Cook's Notes

🕐 TIME: Preparation takes about 20 minutes, baking takes about 35 minutes, plus cooling time.

◻ SERVING IDEA: A pecan half may be placed on top of each square before serving.

If necessary, a little melted chocolate will hold it in place.

▦ COOK'S TIP: Serve with ice cream for a special dessert.

CHOCOLATE SWIRL CHEESECAKE SQUARES

Makes sixteen 2-inch squares

These picture perfect bars are an irresistible combination of melted semisweet chocolate swirled into a cream cheese base.

Crust
1 cup graham cracker crumbs
¼ cup butter of margarine, melted
3 tbsps sugar

Filling
½ cup (3oz) semisweet chocolate chips or pieces
1 package (8oz) cream cheese, softened
¾ cup undiluted CARNATION Evaporated Milk
½ cup sugar
1 egg
2 tbsps all-purpose flour
2 tsps vanilla extract

1. Preheat oven to 300°F. Grease an 8-inch square baking pan.

2. To make the crust, combine cracker crumbs, butter and sugar in a small bowl. Press firmly into bottom of baking pan.

STEP 2

3. For the filling; melt chocolate in a small saucepan over low heat.

4. In blender container, place cream cheese, evaporated milk, sugar, egg, flour and vanilla; process until smooth.

STEP 4

5. Gradually stir ½ cup cheese mixture into melted chocolate. Pour remaining cheese mixture into crust. Pour chocolate mixture over cheese mixture. Swirl mixtures together with knife or spoon to create marbled effect.

STEP 5

6. Bake for 40 to 45 minutes, or until set. Cool in pan on wire rack before cutting. Cover and store in refrigerator.

Cook's Notes

TIME: Preparation takes about 20 minutes, baking takes about 40 minutes, plus cooling.

? VARIATION: Crust may be made with chocolate wafer crumbs or chocolate cookie crumbs instead of graham cracker crumbs.

SERVING IDEA: Place bars in decorative papers and arrange on festive platter for a holiday treat.

LEMON CHEESECAKE BARS

Makes about 18 bars

What could be more delicious – a buttery melt-in-your-mouth base with a layer of creamy-lemon cheese filling, topped with sour cream.

Crust
2 cups all-purpose flour
1 cup butter or margarine, softened
½ cup powdered sugar

Filling
1 package (8oz) cream cheese, softened
2 eggs
⅔ cup undiluted CARNATION Evaporated Milk
½ cup granulated sugar
1 tbsp all-purpose flour
1 tbsp lemon juice
2 tsps grated lemon zest
¾ cup sour cream
Shredded or flaked coconut, toasted (optional)

1. Preheat oven to 350°F.

2. To make the crust, combine flour, butter, and powdered sugar in medium bowl and mix well.

STEP 3

Press lightly into bottom and halfway up sides of 13 x 9 x 2-inch baking dish. Bake for 25 minutes (crust will be only partially baked).

3. To make the filling, place cream cheese, eggs, evaporated milk, sugar, flour, lemon juice and lemon zest in a blender container and blend until smooth.

STEP 4

4. Pour filling into partially-baked crust, and continue to bake for 15 minutes. Cool in pan on wire rack.

5. Spread sour cream over top, then chill. Garnish with toasted coconut, if desired. Cut into bars.

STEP 5

Cook's Notes

⏱ TIME: Preparation takes about 15 minutes, baking takes about 40 minutes, plus cooling.

🍽 COOK'S TIP: For a richer lemon-yellow add 2 to 3 drops of yellow food coloring.

◯ SERVING IDEA: Great for everyday snacking, or place on doily-lined decorative platter for entertaining.

OLD FASHIONED CHERRY COBBLER

Makes about 6 servings

This simple and "homey" dessert which was made popular by early settlers is still a favorite today.

1 cup all-purpose flour
⅓ cup sugar
1 tbsp baking powder
2 tbsps butter or margarine, softened
⅔ cup undiluted CARNATION Evaporated Milk
1¾ cups (14oz can) cherry pie filling
French vanilla ice cream (optional)

STEP 2

1. Preheat oven to 350°F.

2. In large mixer bowl, combine flour, sugar, baking powder, butter and evaporated milk; mix well. Spread batter into 9 x 5-inch loaf dish.

3. Spread cherry pie filling over batter. Bake for 40 to 45 minutes. Serve warm with ice cream, if desired.

STEP 2

STEP 3

Cook's Notes

⏱ TIME: Preparation takes about 5 minutes, baking takes about 40 minutes.

❓ VARIATION: Blueberry or strawberry pie filling may be substituted for cherry pie filling.

⭕ SERVING IDEA: May also be served with sweetened whipped cream.

🍳 COOK'S TIP: For a party pleaser, bake in individual dishes.

LIGHT APRICOT MOUSSE

Makes 4 servings

The great summer flavor of apricots can be enjoyed all year round with this rich, yet simple dessert; and no one will guess that it's virtually fat free.

1 envelope unflavored gelatin
½ cup undiluted CARNATION Evaporated Skimmed Milk
2 cups (16oz can) apricot halves in juice, drained
½ tsp vanilla extract
1 egg white
2 tbsps sugar

1. In medium saucepan, sprinkle gelatin over milk and let stand for 5 minutes. Warm over low heat until gelatin is dissolved.

STEP 1

2. In blender or food processor, purée enough apricots to make 1 cup. (Slice any remaining apricots for garnish.)

3. Stir apricot purée and vanilla into milk mixture. Chill, stirring occasionally, until mixture is thick enough to mound on spoon.

STEP 3

4. In small bowl, beat egg white until soft peaks form. Gradually add sugar. Beat until stiff peaks form and sugar is dissolved. Fold into thickened apricot mixture.

STEP 4

5. Spoon into four 4-ounce dessert dishes. Garnish with remaining apricots, and chill.

Cook's Notes

🕐 TIME: Preparation takes 15 minutes, plus chilling time.

❓ VARIATION: ¼ teaspoon almond extract or various liqueurs may be substituted for the vanilla extract.

▢ SERVING IDEA: Serve in stemmed wine glasses for eye-catching appeal.

🍴 COOK'S TIP: Add a sprig of fresh mint for extra garnish.

BAKED LEMON SPONGE PUDDING
Makes 6 servings

This light and tangy old-time favorite is brought up-to-date with a refreshing raspberry sauce.

Pudding
2 eggs, separated
1 cup underlined CARNATION Evaporated Milk
⅓ cup sugar
⅓ cup all-purpose flour
3 tbsps lemon juice
2 tbsps butter or margarine, melted
2 tsps grated lemon zest
¼ cup sugar

Raspberry Sauce
1½ cups (12oz pack) unsweetened, frozen
    raspberries
¼ cup sugar
Lemon zest (optional)

1. Preheat oven to 350°F.

2. In medium bowl, beat egg yolks with wire whisk. Blend in evaporated milk, ⅓ cup sugar, flour, lemon juice, butter and lemon zest.

STEP 3

3. In small mixer bowl, beat egg whites just until soft peaks form. Gradually beat in ¼ cup sugar, beating just until stiff peaks form and sugar is dissolved. Do not overbeat. Carefully fold into lemon mixture.

4. Spoon into six 6-ounce ungreased baking dishes. Place in 13 x 9 x 2-inch baking pan. Fill baking pan with hot water to 1-inch depth. Bake for 35 to 40 minutes or until light golden brown. Carefully remove dishes from hot water bath.

STEP 4

5. In a small saucepan combine the raspberries and sugar for the sauce. Cook over a medium heat until raspberries are thawed and sugar is dissolved. Pour mixture into blender container and process until smooth. Strain mixture through sieve to remove seeds.

6. Spoon warm raspberry sauce over each pudding, sprinkle with lemon zest if desired, and serve immediately.

Cook's Notes

TIME: Preparation takes about 15 minutes, baking takes about 35 minutes.

SERVING IDEA: Sweetened whipped cream may be added if desired, either in place of, or in addition to the raspberry sauce.

COOK'S TIP: Fresh lemons will release more juice if rolled on a flat surface before squeezing.

VARIATION: Can also be baked in a 1-quart casserole set in pan of hot water.

RICH FUDGE SAUCE

Makes about 3 cups

You can create many dessert variations with this delectable sauce – its great over brownies, ice cream or cake.

½ cup butter or margarine
3 squares (1oz each) unsweetened chocolate
2 cups sugar
1½ cups (12oz can) <u>undiluted</u> CARNATION
    Evaporated Milk
1 tsp vanilla extract

---

2. Gradually add evaporated milk, stirring constantly until mixtures come to a boil.

STEP 2

1. In medium saucepan, melt butter and chocolate over medium heat. Stir in sugar.

STEP 1

3. Remove from heat and stir in vanilla. Serve warm or cold.

STEP 3

Cook's Notes

⌚ TIME: Preparation takes about 5 minutes.

❓ VARIATION: Add chopped nuts or cherries for an additional treat.

INDEX

Photography by Peter Barry
Recipes Styled by Helen Burdett
Designed by Judith Chant
Edited by Jillian Stewart
Project co-ordination by Hanni Penrose